The Magnificent

Survivor

By

Ruth DiDomenico

The Magnificent Survivor
Copyright © 2021 Ruth DiDomenico
All rights reserved.

Interior book design by:
Bob Houston eBook Formatting

Marie Bogdonoff

ACKNOWLEDGMENTS

I would first like to thank Marie Bogdondoff and her husband Rob for allowing me to write this book and providing me with the details and pictures that bring it to life. I am grateful to Sue Roper (President of the Tri County Women Veterans Association) for her help in gathering material and editing, along with her suggestions. I am grateful to Lillie Battle and Heath Davenport for their time and expertise for videotaping participants for material in this book, plus editing, fact checking, and adding comments. I am grateful to Father Gary Kadow (Founder & President of Project SOS-Support Our Soldiers) for his editing and fact checking, plus adding material. All of the above are long serving veterans. It is so heartwarming to feel their fervor and love of country. They all registered respect for Marie, who was never a veteran.

I am grateful to my neighbor Lynn Patterson for help in editing, Chuck Ramburg in keeping my computer obedient, and again grateful to Joyce Scales who has so often saved me from my foibles on the computer.

Finally, heartfelt thanks are necessary to Rick Murcer and his dedicated and tireless work designing the unique cover for this book and completing the final edits for publishing. His contributions were instrumental in completing the final draft and, without them, this book would not have been possible.

Ruth DiDomenico

TABLE OF CONTENTS

Chapter 10

INTRODUCTION

THE MAGNIFICENT SURVIVOR

Hopefully, this book can be a beacon for not only surviving, but prospering, and to add to the understanding of how to find profound joy in a troubled world.

Marie Bogdonoff is the most unlikely person to not only establish the entity Villagers for Veterans, but to run it for the last six years. This is a book written by the most unlikely author, a 91-year-old woman with unresolved splinter femur fractures. It is the year 2020, when the world is on fire in the midst of a worldwide Pandemic caused by the Wuhan China Virus known as Covid 19. This has caused increasing shut down of economies around the world, with resurging traumatic virus outbreaks, resulting in millions of deaths from the unknown and changing characteristics of this virus.

Ruth DiDomenico

Chapter 1

First Memories

Marie's earliest memories were of lying in bed, with a doctor overhead putting needles into her legs to determine where she was feeling. She was paralyzed from the waist down. The paralysis lasted a few weeks but left severe deficiencies. Marie had serious muscle atrophy and fatigue, needing leg braces and crutches to be able to take a few steps. She was only three years old.

Her family consisted of her mother and father as well as an older brother who, even though he was inseparable from her, never came down with the virus. There was no vaccine yet in Bolivia, the country of her birth. Her younger sister arrived a year later. Some of Marie's early memories consisted of her mother ironing clothes to wrap around her legs in order to keep the limbs warm. She also remembers wearing long woolen pants in an effort to help with the poor circulation and the cold that affects those with polio.

Marie attended school, though she could never participate in sports or activities that required strength or flexibility. She did excel academically and was never defined by her disability or limitations. She had a very successful business career later on.

At age ten, it was determined that she would need certain surgeries that were not available in Bolivia. Her parents then sold everything and migrated to the United States. It was here she would have three surgeries at the Hospital of Special Surgery in New York. She was thirteen when she had her last ankle fusion and started living a more normal life.

Marie the early years. She's on the right

Chapter 2

The College Years

Marie attended Queens College in 1973. She began a course of study as a premed student; however, organic chemistry did her in, and she switched to accounting, which came easily to her. She graduated in 1982 with a BA in finance. She was 100 percent self-financed and attended school in the evenings while working full-time during the day. This disciplined lifestyle prepared her for a very demanding career in the automotive business. By the time she retired, Marie was the controller of five car dealerships in New York.

In early 1980, she met her husband, Rob, who always says she was this tiny, four foot ten, ninety-five-pound woman whom he was able to put on his shoulders and carry around, just for fun. In 1984 she gave birth to their only child, Michael. Though it was an uneventful pregnancy, it was an extremely difficult delivery.

Chapter 3

The Work Years

Overall, the next fifteen or so years were fairly normal. After Marie's earlier surgeries she lived a life of few limitations. It was in her mid-forties she started experiencing the onset of what she later learned were beginning symptoms of post-polio sequelae, also known as post-polio syndrome. It is a debilitating muscle weakness that causes great fatigue and pain. Increasingly, it became more difficult to function without the aid of a cane, and later on, forearm crutches. As a typical polio survivor, Marie was a workaholic. Her type A personality equipped her well for her usual fourteen-hour days at work and the raising of her son while maintaining her house in the few hours left.

Raising her son was difficult and probably played an important part in her decision to have only one child. Marie's difficulties with mobility and issues with extreme cold weather started her thinking about possibly moving to warmer weather. Post-polio causes extreme pain, especially during very cold winters.

It was in early 2005 that Marie and two of her close friends visited The Villages in Florida, a fifty-five-plus community, on a weekend girlfriend trip. It immediately appealed to Marie, as it was a great place to navigate without the help of others. In her own words, it was a "Marie friendly" place.

It did not take much for Marie to decide that this was the place where she wanted to retire. Before the weekend was over, she put a deposit on a villa and casually informed her husband that she had purchased their retirement home. Rob was so intrigued by her enthusiasm for this community that he wanted to see what was so amazing about the place. His wife was normally cautious. To exhibit impulsive behavior on such a major purchase was surprising.

This community offered over 3,500 clubs, live entertainment every evening, restaurants, swimming pools, and fifty-nine golf courses. It was truly a paradise. The next time Marie and Rob visited The Villages was to furnish their new home—and this was also the first time Rob would see their new house and future retirement place.

As true villagers, the Bogdanoffs officially retired in 2013 after having upgraded to what was to be their second home in this community. With a warm farewell, her employer gave her a wonderful retirement party as well as a brand new Lexus to enjoy in Florida. To date, she continues a warm relationship with her former employer and often helps in a consultant capacity.

Chapter 4

The Villages

In the year 2013, Marie saw a segment of Bill O'Reilly on his involvement with the Independence Fund and the all-terrain chairs gifted to severely injured veterans in an effort to provide greater independence. She decided fundraising for these veterans might be the answer to her retirement-available time.

Her first fundraiser in April of 2014 raised $12,000 for the Independence Fund. Her second fundraiser was later that year for SGT John Peck, a quadruple amputee who was looking to have a double arm transplant. She raised $11,500 for him and, as a result, was invited to a Christmas party at Walter Reed.

It was here that Marie realized that God had a plan for her.

After meeting fifteen of the most catastrophically injured soldiers, she knew that she would need to dedicate her time to raising money to help injured veterans overcome some of the many challenges they faced as a result of their war wounds. Villagers for Veterans was born. Marie formed a 501(c)3 and called it Villagers for Veterans.

John Peck with Marie and other Veterans

Chapter 5

The Programs: Mobility and Independence

Having many mobility issues herself, Marie knew that helping injured warriors regain some of the independence they lost due to their injuries was front and center. She also learned that women veterans were not recognized or honored for their service; thus, the Orchid Gala Dinners made its debut. Orchard Gala was born from recognition of an injured air force woman veteran who was in a wheelchair as a result of her injuries. Her husband built her a greenhouse and she started to raise orchids as therapy.

At the first Orchid Gala, Jennifer Griffin, a FOX News correspondent, was the keynote speaker. Marie had met Jennifer at a Gary Sinise concert in South Carolina. Marie thought that she could arrange a book-signing event for Jennifer. This was a book that Jennifer and her husband Greg had written during her chemotherapy. At this first Orchid Gala, all the planets were aligned, and the fundraiser raised $140,000 for our nation's veterans. It was a truly amazing evening. Because of the great success of this evening, Bill O'Reilly gave Marie a well-deserved shout out.

Marie with Jennifer Griffin and Friends

Through their connection with the Independence Fund, Marie and Rob were invited to visit the Walter Reed Army Medical Center. It was there Marie met two soldiers with severe burns as well as eleven other soldiers who had suffered catastrophic injuries.

Marie came home with more resolve to help these veterans and was at once at peace with her purpose in life. Spending her time on worthy, productive, and meaningful activities met her life's pattern—that of busy days getting things done, pride in her work, and experiencing the profound joy that comes from serving others.

She had found the secret of successful living—that is, experiencing each day of a purpose-driven life and all of its rewards.

The sleepless nights became the most creative time for future projects.

Chapter 6

Service Dog for Pam Kelly

Pam Kelly is a US Army veteran who served as the first-response combat medic in her unit. In 2002 while training for a deployment to Iraq, she was injured while involved in a sling load operation gone wrong resulting in the load falling and crushing her. This catastrophic event resulted in injuries to her head, multiple spine fractures, and fractures of both shoulders. She lives with a traumatic brain injury (TBI), severe post-traumatic stress disorder (PTSD), and numerous other medical issues. This brave army veteran is now a quadriplegic with only limited use of her left arm.

At an event, Marie took notice of Pam interacting with service dogs and proceeded to ask her why she did not have a service dog–a dog that would not only provide service but a dog that could provide love and assistance, and also one that would improve Pam's ability to function.

Marie found out that a service dog for Pam would have to be specially trained to meet her quadriplegic demands. This specially trained dog can close and open doors, fetch items, answer the phone and bring it to Pam, and turn on and off lights. Marie found an organization that was led by another woman quadriplegic who would be able to train a service dog to meet Pam's needs.

A service dog with the special training both for Pam and the dog would cost about $17,000. Undaunted, Marie set about forming a $25 fundraising breakfast at Evans Prairie Country Club. Her arrangements were that the restaurant would donate the food. One Air Force Veteran donated $5,000 for the cause as a charitable donation to the 501(c)3. That event raised the sum needed and became the inspiration to help Pam obtain an adapted house in the future. The estimated cost would be in the range of $400,000.

Service dog for Pam

Marie planned a series of events starting with a 5K walk at The Villages polo field. "I walk for Pam" raised $19,000. Marie also organized monthly Bingo games, dances, and entertainment shows–at which events additional funds were raised through the sale of flags, caps, 50/50 raffle tickets, tickets to future events, etc. Marie also hosted themed dinners and wine tasting events.

Pam Kelly showed her deep appreciation for Marie Bogdonoff in January 2019 during the groundbreaking ceremony for her new home in The Village of Orange Blossoms Gardens.

By January of 2020, The American Legion Auxiliary hosted a housewarming event that welcomed Pam into her new house within The Villages. Most participating women veterans brought useful housewarming presents. Pam, who once said, "I am an Army sergeant who doesn't cry," teared up that day as she talked about what Marie Bogdonoff means to her.

She said, "If I had a second mother, I would want it to be Marie. She is my family and it will be that way until the day I die and beyond. She has changed my life."

Marie reciprocated by saying she considers Pam as part of her family and is thrilled with how Pam has changed over the years they have known each other. "She has become a full person in the sense she feels that her life is worth living," Marie said. "I think this situation has made her realize that she will never be alone, not in this community anyway. She does not have to worry about anything because these people here who have her back."

Marie and Pam

In November of 2019 Pam took part in a Flightless Village honor flight. Honor Flight Tri-State offers a program called the Flightless Honor Flight for veterans who are wheelchair bound or who can no longer fly due to health reasons. They are met by the Honor Flight Ambassador ground crew and taken to a checkpoint. A special room waits where the Ambassador treats them to an Honor Flight "virtual tour" of the monuments, including movies of real tours, possible local tour to the American Legion and Eisenhauer Center, special presentation of souvenirs, and light refreshments. The veteran experiences the welcome ceremony, color guard, bagpipes, mail call, and about two hours later, they exit the auditorium.

Chapter 7

All Women Honor Flight

The Honor Flight Network is a national network of independent hubs working together to honor our nation's veterans with an all-expense paid trip to the memorials in Washington D.C., a trip many of the veterans may not otherwise be able to take. Villages Honor Flight Inc. was formed as an official hub of this network in July 2011 and provides trip opportunities for veterans living in Lake County, Sumter County, Marion County, Citrus County, or Hernando County. Four trips a year, consisting of 40 veterans each trip, are coordinated and executed by Villages Honor Flight. These trips are highly coveted. Veterans are selected by age, and currently include veterans who served from WWII to the Korean War, and through to Vietnam and Operation Desert Storm/Desert Shield. From 2011 through 2019, only .04% of the selected veterans were women.

The Tri County Women Veterans (established 1999), a group of over 200 women veterans, requested that Villages Honor Flight (VHF) consider an All-Women Veteran Honor Flight but were told that because VHF had several hundred veterans already signed up and waiting to be manifested on future flights, it would not be fair for the women to jump ahead of those who had been waiting for years. However, Villages Honor Flight staff did agree to coordinate an All-Women Veteran Honor Flight as a special add-on flight if the women could raise approximately $50,000.

In the fall of 2019, the Tri County Women Veterans reached out to Marie and her Villages for Veterans organization, requesting the organization serve as their fiscal agent, since Tri County Women Veterans is not a 501(c)3 organization. The women veterans also asked for assistance in coordinating fundraising events and opportunities to finance this special flight.

During the two-month signup for this special flight (November-December 2019), close to 100 women veterans signed up for the flight. As a result, the flight became a Charter Flight and grew to accommodate 60 women veterans and 60 guardians, many of whom are also women veterans. The fund-raising goal was then raised to $100,000. Fundraising, which had become a partnership between Villagers for Veterans and the Tri County Women Veterans, began the second week of January 2020 with a weekly Martini tasting held at Bonifay Country Club, and monthly Bingo events held at Wildwood Community Center. Additional fundraisers would include concerts and breakfast events. Women veterans and members of Villagers for Veterans also solicited and acquired many individual and corporate sponsorships.

Then Covid-19 hit, and everything shut down, at least initially. As the weeks moved on and guidance was provided regarding wearing masks, social distancing, and the safety of outdoor activities, Marie made arrangements to restart smaller weekly bingo games and weekly trivia nights outside in the breezeways (patios) at the Bonifay and Belle Glade Country Clubs. From April through mid-September, women veterans were on duty at the clubs selling bingo cards, 50/50 raffle tickets, flags, hats, masks, and tickets for upcoming events. In September 2020, during the annual Orchid Gala Festival honoring women veterans, it was announced that $100,000 had been raised for the flight and was "mission accomplished."

Joe Hambright, who serves as chairman of the board of Villages Honor Flight said that he was amazed at how fast Villagers for Veterans in partnership with the Tri County Women Veterans raised the money for the extra flight. This extra flight will not push any veteran back on any other waiting list.

Lisa Walters, who serves as vice president of operations for the group and will be the flight director on the all-women flight stated that this flight will make history when it takes place. The donation is the largest her organization has ever received. The next event is tentatively scheduled for the Spring of 2022.

Marie with Tri County Women Veterans

Chapter 8

Veterans and Their Families Who Live in the Ocala Forest

One of Marie's side projects as a result of the Covid Pandemic is assisting Project SOS-Support Our Soldiers, that provides for homeless veterans and their families who live in the Ocala Forest.

The Ocala Forest is a large area of land with a mixture of private and public lands spanning four counties extending all the way from Ocala to Leesburg, Florida. It consists of up to 430,000 acres of land. Marie assisted Project SOS by helping to support homeless veterans and their families with some funds, food, clothing, and infant and children products, in addition to meeting other specific needs.

At Halloween time, she put out a message to her list of supporters to bring goodie bags for the children of veterans who live there. She collected so many bags that she had to cancel a scheduled meeting at her house because there was no room for the participants.

Project SOS (Support Our Soldiers) is managed by an Episcopalian Priest, Father Gary Kadow. Gary is an air force, Vietnam Veteran who is passionate about his fellow veterans. He says there are approximately 6,000 people (seasonally) living in the forest with increasing numbers. The veteran count is less predictable.

Father Kadow maintains that when the first veterans arrived, they valued their privacy. Most of these veterans live on social security and Veterans disability funds. Living rent free and mortgage free allows them to buy food, beer, pet food, warm clothing, and needed supplies. As the numbers grow, sanitation and safety become more of a problem. Some veterans are suffering from depression and PTSD. Some live in campers, some tents, treehouses, broken down vehicles, and other makeshift housing. He and Marie complement their projects and he is so appreciative of her contributions to their joint missions. More information is available at www.projectsos.org.

Ocala Forest recipients for Veterans food bags

Chapter 9

Round Up

A summary of Marie's fundraising projects over the years includes an amazing total of $1,565,500 for many veterans programs. This number includes the mobility and independence program with a sum of $672,807, which includes 39 track chairs, numerous adapted sport wheelchairs, all-terrain vehicles and bikes, and three electric scooters.

Track chairs Provide an Amazing Service

Service dog programs amount to $72,501 which includes sponsoring ten service dogs, sponsoring two graduations, and helping veterans with some veterinary bills for their service dogs.

Service Dogs ready to love on their people

Workshops for veterans and assisting with PTSD programs came to $124,655 which includes equine therapy, art and music as well as adaptive sport outings and special sponsorships to organizations with similar missions.

Equine Therapy is very effective

There are also retreats such as the Spartan weekend retreats in The Villages.

These retreat weekends are events to help veterans connect with other veterans or get a battle buddy. It is an effort to bring awareness to veterans and first responder suicide. The NY Fire Dept 343 provides a sword forged of Trade Center Steel where veterans and first responders take a pledge to reach out to their buddies before attempting to hurt themselves. The weekend is set up with all kinds of activities that bring camaraderie.

Spartan weekend

Also supported has been Camps for Heroes, an outdoor retreat that supports veterans with PTSD. This as well as other programs assisting veterans in need, including Project SOS, raised $167,728.

ADA Smart Home for Sgt Pam Kelly came to $408,857.

Women Veteran Honor Flight came to $100,000.

Veterans in need and in crisis came to $167,728.

Assisting veterans with food, furniture, appliances, and small house repairs.

Fundraisers for specific veterans such a Sgt John Peck.

Villagers for Veterans also has money in the general fund in case it needs to support something outside of regular programs.

Too many other fundraisers and projects to list.

For example: In October of 2016 fundraising events included segments of some of the fun times, like the moments with Gary Sinise. Gary is the actor who played Lt. Dan in Forrest Gump. In October of 2016, a red-carpet event and a 5K run was scheduled. Each event benefits the Gary Sinise Foundation.

Gary and Marie

The event featured entertainment by different clubs from The Villages that put theatrical skits representative of the eras covered in the movies, and the 5K run was appropriately called: "Run Forrest, Run." Gary's foundation serves our nation by honoring our defenders, veterans, first responders, their programs designed to entertain, educate, inspire, strengthen and build communities.

Marie Bogdonoff, the founder and President of Villagers for Veterans, shared a special backstage moment with Gary Sinise in February 2019 at the Savannah Center where he talked about his bestselling book "Grateful American: A Journey from Self to Service." Each member received a copy, which details Sinise's life story from troubled kid to Hollywood star to activist for veterans.

In October 2019, Sinise was back in The Villages with his Lt. Dan Band, rocking Florida's Friendliest Hometown in front of a packed house at Lake Sumpter Landing. Sinise formed the 13-piece band in 2003 as an arm of the Gary Sinise Foundation with a goal of entertaining troops performing at USO shows and raising money to help disabled veterans.

The foundation now raises in excess of Thirty-Million dollars annually.

Gary Sinise with band

Those who know Marie won't be surprised to learn that after the presentation of the Villages Honor Flight donation, she wasted no time in diving into her next projects. Villagers for Veterans hosted a USO-themed event at Paquette's Historical Farmall Tractor Museum in Leesburg to benefit Project SOS-Support Our Soldiers, Inc. Raising money for transition housing for homeless female veterans in Lake County is also high on the agenda.

As I said earlier, I applaud Marie and her Villagers for Veterans for all they have done to help veterans in need. They have made a huge difference in countless lives. I have no doubt they will continue to do the same thing for many other veterans in the years to come.

A Gary Sinise Foundation ambassador is scheduled to be here for additional events. Marie looks forward to working with the Gary Sinise Foundation and introducing this wonderful organization to our wonderful community. Marie said, "No one knows better the generosity of Villagers than I. They have been extremely supportive and generous in my fundraisers that benefit our nation's heroes who have sacrificed so much for our freedom."

Awareness of the huge challenges faced by families of wounded warriors was highlighted in the book "The Mighty Moms and Wounded Warriors of Walter Reed" written by Dava Guerin and Kevin Forris.

When Marie was at Walter Reed, she met some of these moms. Marie said, "I bought the book and, when I got home, I sobbed and sobbed. I contacted the woman who wrote the book and asked her to come here."

Villagers were able to meet some of the wounded veterans and their moms at a book signing. "Folks met some real tough kids and amazing moms," Marie added.

Marie and Rob may have a lot on their plates, but they said none of it could even be attempted if it weren't for their good-hearted volunteers. "I have a lot of really good friends who worked really hard to make it all happen," Marie said. "I'd like to thank each and every one of them for their support."

Marie and Family

Chapter 10

What's It All About?

What Marie displays in her life is that no matter what you are dealt, you can overcome all and experience a profound joy every day that you live by learning the secrets of her successful life.

Pain teaches us that we can endure the hardships in our lives. It is sometimes called "The gift of hardship." We can transform our suffering into wisdom and positive energy. The drive to make a difference in the world is initially related to meaning, a sense that what is happening to you, and around you, matters in some way. Marie answers the question by asking, "What future would I like to see happen?"

1. First is to endure pain and increase endurance, see and experience life's satisfactions.

2. Generate positive emotions and actively decrease negative emotions.

3. Generate an ongoing sense of flourishing rather than being hapless.

4. Focus on the joy around you and ignore the sad distractions.

5. Foster a willingness to do what is truly good for the wellness of others.

6. Be a part of something bigger than yourself, set in motion a purpose driven life.

7. Live in harmony with nature.

8. Have the heart of a servant and the spirit of a warrior.

9. Always bring your best self to the world.

10. Put your faith in God, family, and yourself so that everything is working for the betterment of all.

11. We are truly here for a short time, so go out and live the life you have imagined. It is really a wonderful journey.

Our bodies are matter in motion vibrating at an intensity that light does not pass through. It is the free-flowing energy going into and out of a living cell that keeps this cell nourished and healthy. When energy goes out of a cell and is blocked by, say anger in all of its forms, the cost to the body is inflammatory. Examples could be arthritis, fasciitis, gastritis, pancreatitis. When energy is blocked coming into a cell by fear in all of its forms, the cost is degenerative for lack of nutrients. Examples are sarcoma, osteoma, blastoma.

There are six principles to use when life is challenging.

1. When you are feeling stressed or down, go out and do something for someone quick. This is energy out, but more important, by thinking beyond your own miserable current circumstances, you diminish your misery because you are changing focus.

2. Do something for yourself. You need to put energy in to continue putting out. It is okay to pamper yourself with your favorite pleasures like going out to lunch or dinner with friends, go to a movie, have a massage, read a book. This is energy in.

3. Produce something. This could be writing a book or an encouraging letter to a friend, make a garden, paint a picture, compose a song. This is energy out.

4. Learn something, read a book, take piano lessons, attend a lecture. This is energy in.

5. Love something. This can be a person, a cat or dog, flowers, a beautiful sunset, your house. This is energy out.

6. Let someone love you. This is probably the hardest, because it makes you vulnerable. This is energy in.

Putting it all together, doing something for someone or for you is for the BODY.

Learning or producing something is for the MIND.

Love something or letting someone love you is for the SPIRIT.

Putting it all together covers all the bases of Body, Mind, and Spirit and leaves little room for misery.

Look at hardships as a gifts, for the struggle makes you strong and allows God to work in all of us.

Ruth DiDomenico

AUTHOR NOTE:

The Magnificent Obsession was written by Lloyd C. Douglas in 1929. It was the story of a wealthy playboy named Robert Merrick. He lived a carefree lifestyle and was responsible for the death of an eccentric but beloved surgeon. After reading about this doctor's productive life, Robert was forced to reevaluate his own life. He changes his lifestyle of personal pleasure to that of becoming an anonymous philanthropic as an obsession. He had found the formula to profound joy in service to others.

I read this book in my early twenties. It had a strong influence on my formation during a time when I was finding out who I was and who I wanted to become.

Through the years it was a source of decisions going forward. As a new member of the Women's Veterans Association, I met Marie Bogdonoff while volunteering at fundraising events for an all-Women's Honor Flight. Marie had a lot to say about everything which was surprising as she was short in stature and on two crutches but her spirit was obvious.

When I learned her story, I wanted to write THE MAGNIFICENT SURVIVOR. The book became almost an obsession for me so here it is.

Although from different origins, both Marie and Robert had both found the secret of living with profound joy in the service to others. The story of her life is that of transforming the gift of hardship into the lifestyle described in this book.

The struggle makes you strong.

Author Ruth DiDomenico

Made in the USA
Monee, IL
19 May 2021